a study of frustration

poems

dillon thomas jones

word west press | brooklyn, ny

copyright © 2021 dillon thomas jones

all rights reserved. no part of this book may be used or reproduced in any manner whatsoever without written permission from the publisher except in the case of brief quotations embodied in critical articles or reviews. for more information, contact word west press.

isbn: 9781736947708

published by word west in brooklyn, ny.

first us edition 2021.
printed in the usa.

www.wordwest.co

cover & interior design: word west.
cover photo: abner tunchez

introduction
   tonya

methods
   four months shy of twenty seven
   eight to ten
   six
   twentytwo
   burned letter to birth mother: rolep
   nine
   nine
   four
   eighteen nineteen twenty one twenty six
   twenty one
   twenty
   burned letter to birth mother: divine intervention
   almost twenty
   twenty three
   burned letter to birth mother: bedtime storytime

findings
   *
   burned letter to birth mother: one more question
   sevenish
   mid twenties
   thirty or so
   burned letter to birth mother: my private investigator suggested i write down all the questions i want to ask you
   twenty five
   fourteen

twentysix
sixteen or so
burned letter to birth mother: tell my father if you see him
thirty two
six
less than zero to five

limitations
burned letter to birth mother: when i was five my mother told me all about you
burned letter to birth mother: bedtime storytime
burned letter to birth mother: blink

recommendations
thirteen
twenty nine
twenty eight

conclusion
burned letter to birth mother: if youre reading this its too late
elegy

tonya

couldnt stop making you making you making you

figured you were gods punishment
for being fast again figured
you felt in how my heart beat i
never wanted to make you

& thats why you didnt kick me
during month four figured
you might die inside me
gods punishment or you
spiteful because i didnt want you

when the lady said
we cant find a heartbeat
during month five i said
cut this thing out of me but
the lady said this happens sometimes
lets wait & see

i figured it was you or god
spiteful playing you were dead
like a dog trick i never liked

it was that night
maybe somehow you remember
i unwrapped my hair singing
someday ooh someday
the one you gave away
will be the only one
youre wishing for

couldnt stop making you making you making

you kicked my kidney so hard
i peed my blue electric leggings
couldnt stop

*

momma spit me out one night in cleveland
ohio a mile or so from the hospital
wanted my first sight to be the stars
shining on a summer night in ohio

momma say why they so pearly
she cant remember her daddy told her
cherokee girls born in starlight attract
all kinds of cosmic favor from the gods

daddy said one god is all his flock need
to concern ourselves with we were lucky
daddy was there to shepherd us
in the name of the lord god

what we need to know about starlight
or tree gods or baths in rivers
we got a shower under a roof
 hand me your prayers ill deliver them
onto our lord god the big big man in the sky
big big man of our one room shack
nailed & hammered out of dead
gods daddy felled himself

built a roof as sky stars made of
light bulbs over my crib lighting
mommas mouth as she sang
a song about burning
bright nights like the night
she spit me out in cleveland ohio

*

tamarra drove me to capital care
womens center left a message
with a medicine woman on parson
brought over a lighter & brand
new metal hangers

t&t tam & ton the two-tone tomboys
me & tamarra go way way way back
since kid days girls called her black
as the blackest shadow black
as the blackest coal white santa
stuck in her stocking

i brought ice buckets
for her red knuckles
kissed her brow after
she fought pinky for
telling the whole squad
i was pregnant again

why should i give of myself
if i never meant to make you
why swell up until we both go
red

tamarra brought instruction manuals for
time travel machines that go back
to the moment your daddy started &
make him stop make his daddy stop
my daddy stop

the photons went haywire
the womens center closed due to
a firebomb tamarra burned
the tip of a metal hanger

four months shy of twenty seven

grey thunderclouds rumble
engorged alarm clocks stirring old aches
scars she put in your sternum
years ago healed ribs disguise
weather beaten blue bruising

maybe yes there is enough time for
a short loop through schenley park

tall white woman short white man
jog alongside a doberman pincher
the usual suspects
gleaming white fangs
slit your wrist someday

something to explain to a lover
beneath an oak tree
by the gazebo a doe grazes with her fawn
rain shine or snow they graze here
above the tall grasses

how many years since
your *crunch krstap kraaak*
scattered them
two at least
sing your names for them

11   *methods*

superabundant clouds overwhelm
thunder forks your notes
what aches is burning dully now
what rumbles above darkly
rumbles inside as darkly
the fawn stumbles into his mother
without looking she flicks a hoof
in its chest you must run now

to catch the fawn
who is teeter tottering
ten yards away
close enough
hear old aches
in the thud
her hoof makes

a twitch in your lower back
becomes a dead sprint because
the fawn still staggers
you catch her him it
bucks & bays against your chest
lurching for the tall grass
grubby hoofs *whackwhackwhack*
your groin your chin

here comes the does lowered head
into your ribcage
leaves you on your knees
a god says to the clouds
let the tall grass blades
bear the loads you carry
& raindrops fill your
eyes with black light

pitter patter angel kisses
if only

gods grace loosens your grip
the fawn its fluttering butterfly heartbeat
rejects you as lord & savior

barrels through a wall of glutinous grass
the doe pursues without a backwards glance
purple prongs cut up the grey soaked sky
the rain floods evergreen hoof prints

the ache in your bones aches
like the itch you cannot domesticate
pitter patter notes beat shoulder
blade forehead teeth brings to mind
a window in a song

headlights glance off your body
your silhouette freezes in periphery
restless fingers clutching its own arms
hunched over when lightening relents
clouds hasten on

eight to ten

*my mother said dont raise your voice
never run in public
dont go south of twentieth & ames
if you get pulled over
say oh hello officer
how are you
oh im so sorry
thank you*

*dont make such a fuss
dont look at me like that
dont pout dont forget
people only care about themselves
dont interrupt when im talking
dont talk back you drug victim
dont lie*

*never tell anyone what happens here
its our secret they wont understand*

*truth is no one cares about you
dont forget that*

*dont forget you are a clump of dead brown skin
a clump of black pubic hair clogging the drain
like the tongue of smoke from an extinguished fire
one senses your brightest days are behind you*

*people stare they shake their heads sigh
what a shame*

*dont forget theres always someone
smarter than you better looking etc
make yourself so small
no one can see you
but me*

so im small as the droplets of
water she shook from her hands
like a good boy im always saying
*how are you please im so sorry
thank you so much*

six

to see what will happen
molly goldberg finds a rock
& writes MOLLY GOLDBERG
in chalk white on your thigh

to see if skin changes color
she hawks a big one wipes
her blackboard clean accepts
jimmys james crown of dandelions

in the bathtub you pretend
youre white as jesse in *free willy*
diving inside a ring of pink bubble fire
trapping a rubber whale wailing for
drumming helicopter wings
the ring of fire encroaches
will a harness spill from heaven
in time no no
boy & fish burn
you rise glistening brown
but not for long

thigh too meaty
wrist mostly bone any way
start there
break skin scoop
the brown the pink gunk
bore to bone
become a boy who was
his own angel
hand spilled from heaven

like molly goldbergs gamble with a rock
beneath the monkey bars
little bit of spit
little bit of elbow grease

twentytwo

the problem with your hand is
theres no way to tell
what itll do next

any light tap on
my shoulder blade
might get bloody later
can you say it wont
for sure

you cant
thats the problem
consider the issue of
intimate play
fondling as it were
that may devolve
gradually into
wonton roughhousing
your hands heavy
persistent

i can say no
no thank you
but when that doesnt matter
i climb ten thousand feet
& watch you
happening to my body
even if its only a little fondling
i bolt

youll never know im gone

no no sorry
i dont believe youre different
or whatever
yes yes i know

this behavior suggests
an obsession with control
plus an aversion to &
discomfort with physical
slash emotional intimacy
despite my stated desire
to be known seen understood
loved etc & to know see
understand love etc

i watch you watch my hands
while you bite your nails
i watch you close your eyes when
something happens to us
you say for sure it wont
but you cant say that
you cant say that

burned letter to birth mother: roleplay

my mother plays doctor
slips a bitter white hand beneath
my baby blue baby blanket

i watch *m*a*s*h* while she works
testicles like golden
baoding balls doing figure eights
on red fingernail tips

korean kids squirm
on hawkeyes lap
i squirm
lift her hand
say *stop*

she finishes
when she finishes

i watch *will & grace*
frasier & *m*a*s*h*
praying the *franzia*
sunset blush knocks her flat

these days im a dead patient
who wakes up paralyzed
from the neck down

i go stiff in the dark if
a womans breath is *franzia*
sunset blush

red fingernails fumble
under a baby blue baby blanket
i grow stiff

nine

todays order
gordo christian
oona seb ant zach
jessica lou frankie

i review the rules
no handlebars no helmets
your final form is scored
a bone break beats a blood leak
beats a bruise size & color are scored

orange beats purple beats blue
red is best danielle proved
pain is easily exaggerated
if your screams summon an adult
you will not be asked to play again

as far as form goes
best to follow gavins example
maintain a straight back
hips in line
arms winged
neck high
halfway down the hill
you will want to scream
resist this urge

dont decide your final contortions
before gravity brings you down
excessive crying will be penalized

olivia owns the high score
down the hill in eleven seconds
a snow angel flip over the handlebars
cracked vertebrae
concussed
blood dripping from
her earlobe
thirteen point five

the first to make it look easy

nine

on good morning america
one of the billowing twin towers
looks like my mom hard shifting gears
smoking a camel cigarette late for school

just after the second morning bell
a plane big as a horse fly
zips into tower number two
principal mitchel gasps but

im not fooled by clumsy special effects
fireballs like that only happen in die hard
mom says their hearts will burst
before they survive the fall

no morning announcements
mrs woodland turns on cnn
says terrorists attacked america
but were safe in nebraska in fact
president bush is on his way
it is so safe shes crying

she cries the whole day we watch cnn
says everything will be okay
only brown nosers tommy
john & tabitha believe her

todays lesson is what links all americans
big small black white etc
an opaque coil of tension
strung through the lower belly

on the playground blacktop
we played towers & terrorists
tommy john & tabitha are
the two planes slash terrorists
i am the first tower smoking
my mothers camel cigarette

*

daddy always say
woman is submissiveness incarnate

daddy always say
no woman shall teach nor
exercise authority over a man
she is to remain quiet

me & mama are quiet
when daddy in the house
sitting with godly dignity
waiting for daddy to finish
a sermon hell deliver sunday

at night he practices on his back
in my bed promises hell save me
if i continue in faith love & holiness

when i asphyxiate his throat
i look him in his eyes
he shudders

four

their collective white body
stirs where my spine curves
where my shoulders slope
under a blue napping mat
wrapped in black without
air

just a game to them
of which i am folly
its not my fault
i know

were i fleeter of foot or
smaller of lung
then

i could escape or
die quickly instead
i lived on occasionally
paralyzed neck down

its not my fault
theres a thrashing
at the edge of my vision
a kind of blackness
encloses at a studied pace

those white boys showed me
breath becomes black dust

becomes a blooming patchwork
of spangled sunflower light

i am grateful.

eighteen nineteen twenty one twenty six

first time was freshman year halloweekend
i was abc skinned Michael Jackson wearing a thriller jacket
drank a fifth of vodka dived in capitol beach lake

frankenstein & cleopatra pulled me out
just some silly drunk shit is what everyone thought
oh well then that time tailgating at iowa state
slammed two four lokos inside ten minutes

pissed myself in a lawn chair
pat & geoff dragged my heap of bones
two miles back to phi delta theta
god bless sweet frat boys lush carpets &
david the chaperone saying
you arent allowed outside
i said good if you let me out
i wont come back

couldnt say ill kill myself
needed to maintain some ongoing
flexibility to change my mind
laid down on that lush carpet
thinking better luck next time dillon

next time was every single night
in xian that summer drinking *baijiu*
pleading with cab drivers to swerve
into oncoming traffic for me alas
i know now my life is my burden alone

nicole fucked her ex an excuse to
mix everclear with stepping off a balcony
i never thanked ali for her timely pleas
my lesson learned was no witnesses

a year or so later two am
i laid down on haymarket bridge
after enough *franzia* & *xanax*
to finish off what was left of me
in maybe ten more minutes
an insomniac discovered me
five minutes later with charm
i convinced a paramedic a nurse
a doctor walter & becky i just
couldnt handle my alcohol
not since I was eleven ive
been begging god to send
me sleepwalking femoral
artery first into my mothers
favorite steak knife

recently it clicked why
people do heroin happily
reporting this to friends
has caused alarm
i reassure them
what im saying is
the first time i do heroin
will be the last obviously

ill go when the time comes
dump my ashes in papio creek

twenty one

my friends are real cool black
men who like chocolate cigars &
dollar store vodka

i blab my white friend
dave slapped me
they wont meet my eyes

instead of gutting him
with one of amandas
steak knives or
peeling back his scalp
with a bottle opener
like they say they wouldve done
i sprinted six blocks
tears streaming
pissed myself asleep

wed split a water bottle of jack daniels
plus i said *of fucking course*
you want to be white
dont say such stupid shit or
something i think hurt his feeling
so i left if id stayed

i wouldve killed him i think
no
no
i wouldve apologized wept

you know what im saying
no
they dont know what im saying
ashamed i let a white man
put his hands on me

but daves just a boy
& im just a boy
it seems to me
the problem was
i wasnt really listening to him

you know what im saying
no
they dont know what im saying

a white man backhands a black man
dont see whats so complicated

i think the issue was my framing of
the problem i put to them
my real cool black men friends
i shouldve said sorry

please look in my eyes

twenty

im in a room on fire
roasting skin up my nose
its not my fault

door locked from the outside
window sealed from inside i see
white blue breeze humping honeysuckle

& no one came no one comes no one will
look in my eyes & you wont see me
trying to put my shoulder through the glass

with my smoke for bones my blackened mind
& no one came no one comes no one will
& if by some chance you notice get curious

& come knocking itll be the wrong door
a sign will read i dont want to be rescued
i want to put my shoulder through this glass

im in a room on fire
burning for what for who
& its not my fault
its not my fault

burned letter to birth mother: divine intervention

she almost said ill pass
says god moved her to say
ill take him really
she wanted to adopt

a hispanic girl to name katherine
gloria for her late mother but
when god speaks
you better listen

i want to trade places with katherine gloria
even if yesterday she got tboned or
minutes ago drowned in lake erie

even if her heart transplant is failing or
her plane is falling out of the sky
i lick my lips imagining
the end of my suffering

i hear my mothers voice

i almost said ill pass
you selfish ungrateful
boy i wanted a hispanic girl
katherine gloria

almost twenty

i watch white starlight
beat back black water
in the night sky drifting
on smoky pavement
blue lights flashing

like those cerulean eyes
glancing through sunlight
shafts caught glistening
in the rivets lining
my golden forehead

slouching across
the green lawns of
nebraska university
boxedin by towering
european white birches
abutting sunflower clusters
butterfly bushes waving
to the beat of the breeze
whipped up by a current
of searching minds atop
pale bodies boxedin
soldering shut
black feelings

i embrace reject embrace
reject as it suits me till
i can stomach a handful of
xanax with franzia supine
on a cool concrete raft

i can see what comes next
an uncoiling of light unto
light unto light framed
& centered gentle yet firm
like a weighted blanket of
whirlpooling dark
pockmarked blue sirens
invidious fingernails

scraping

twenty three

there my golden bronze mass
suspended in gunmetal fog
unbound

hands raised blued
bruises cloaked in
whispering smoke
silence rings impossibly

i consider my attempts
to expedite my life
toward another kind
strongarm fate you could say

i decide the times fit for it

a nice rest in this bed of grey
potential that vanishes
that eats course corrects
breathing errors

the stone in my chest
there it goes
slick with what stuck to me
soon to be indistinguishably
wet in a wet thing
no longer the center it held

burned letter to birth mother: bedtime storytime

i fetch the *franzia chardonnay*
from her bedroom closet select
the monster at the end of this book

at the kitchen table hunched
my mother smokes herself a white garland
she reads & we howl at elmos

indifference to grovers panicky pleas
i beg to hear it again & again she obliges
so long as I keep her pink cup full

she slumps over i love her like this
red rimmed blue eyes shut snores
harmonize with the cicadas shrieking

in the bent grass behind the black screen door
the falling sunlight gleams & glances
off her pink corn-fed teeth

years after the last bits of sunlight die
i hear mad howls in blue bloodshot eyes
hide the *franzia* under her winter coats
wearing an ugly glint i haul her to bed

*

daddy left for months
came back
tucked me into bed
whispering

*submit yourself unto
me as unto the lord*

i listened to mama snore
twenty of her short quick
steps down the hallway
daddy laid with his wide
brown hands in silence
like he commanded or else

he would leave &
never come back again
so shhhh be silent
so i was silent

four years every night
i heard thunder in the hallway
naked before he blocked
the doorway he framed
as a young man with wide
shoulders mamma still loves
to watch mend the roof
silent save the rare purr
she lets go when daddy

has extra cash from the till
at church rubbing her big
deacon mans wide stole
bearing shoulders soft
whisper in his ear

thank you lord god
almighty for ministering
our family please
dont leave us

again daddy says
every house need a man of god
submit yourself unto me
as unto the lord

burned letter to birth mother: one more question

did my father rape me into you
is that why you gave me up

did you see his nose in my nose
his eyes in my eyes did my cries
remind you too much of your own

is that why you gave me up
was i a shrieking memento of
a man you hoped to forget
an uninvited guest
finally thrown out
say its so

tell me you couldnt love
a child you didnt want

are my rights your love forfeit
if my father raped me into you
say its so

ill appeal

*

daddy always say hes the roof over our head
the skirts i wear mamas hotcakes
& my golden skin

daddy hummed *golden lady golden*
lady id like to go there go there
go there when i was a girl
spilling his whisky

washing my jheri curl daddy always
say i owe him the love boys give me
because my skin sunshine bright
looking like a lemon lollipop
is that what ill taste

golden lady id like to go there
go there go there on his knee
my lullaby before bed
tamarra always say golden skin
blesses you with life a shade easier

if we could return & exchange blessings
i would choose hazelnut skin
more shade less love i didnt want

im ashamed of your golden skin
i hear daddy sing
golden lady golden lady

sevenish

soon the first firefly will light up
cicadas warm their purring throats
grasshoppers fuck themselves silly

the cheeky sun looking dangerous
in silk a blood orange nightgown
soon enough all will be blue silence

but first an appreciation of the horizon
free forever changing its hue
this evening its seams are lavender

& my lips bloodied by orange
fingernails seem lavender too how
can i keep my new colors forever

before a white noise calls supper is ready
before i black out unlatching her black iron door
i peel away stitch together layer after layer of

lavender dazzled jaundice by
radioactive fire fly light
too late her white noise blacks me out again
black gunk under my fingernails again
grasshoppers dead

mid twenties

inside a room a shadowy figure i know blows raspberries
piecing together charred remains of memories
not knowing the deathbed image is
myriad mercifully brief cracks of light

at least thats what i think toils
in this hothouse body with no doorknob
or peekaboo window
just a sense i have of things as they are
im not an artist really or an architect
got a weak stomach for stories

a lover of the sun hooking fuchsia flourishing an uncompromising line
& of raindrops that split loam coated fingernails
on this is it a winter or fall day without snow leaves
or the sun that grey face covering this golden bronze mug

the truth i suspect is dressed in a shade of
red my eyes cannot show me as presently constituted
best have them out rinsed vigorously under cold water
for fifteen seconds like mouth chocolates
or something else

you there
come up with new names
for what i see

pin back these heavy lids of mine
ill have these lenses poison pricked with light
a long winded way of saying
ill believe its a drum when
i feel the air it strums

another way of not saying
that which is true everyone knows
this silly room in my head
whose texture is myriad
mercifully brief cracks of light

one flashing this woman i saw through on the corner of
michigan & grand in between visions of red blue bleed-
ing
across a dingy black background

you wearing what will get you through
the blustery winter day in chicago
wheat timberlands black long johns
a heavy looking brown carhatt jacket
by the walgreens i think under
the corrugated shadow of
a thundering el station

you know how to ask in stilted
spanish *tiene algún cambio que me pueda dar*
french *avez-vous un changement de rechange*
german *hast du etwas kleingeld*
large peets coffee cup
halfway full of silver
copper green

thought you wouldnt notice
my loafers pick up the pace
i see you brother i see you
do you remember all faces of black
men who pretended they didnt see
those royal blue fingernails against honey
walnut skin or hear in your voice
something worth a glance of recognition
confirmation of a certain kinship
black men who forever carry
an enduring shame with the same sonic
dimensions of your chilly voice

i wish now to have registered your face
surely i must have its profile somewhere
in this silly room in my head whose texture
is myriad mercifully brief cracks of light

all i see is a plume of white smoke
coiling out of his bright pink mouth
in between visions of red blue bleeding
across a dingy black background

the black dot of pen ink
where the community needle
entered a reedy blue vein
his caramel skin looks beaten
violet black as the core of a wilting
sunflower on one of junes hottest
& whitest days we met again
after how many years

lost in the glassy green flecks
in eyes scanning my closed golden

bronze face trying to pinch a memory
wrinkled fingers still thicker than mine
tugging neck length matted dreadlocks
with yellow nails split by accident

yet more fingers trap a rouge itch
along the inner curve of a leftside rib bone
emeka the fleet footed boy who marked me
on the pitch dogged smiling always
the first in line to extend a hand lose or win
still stands a little close for my comfort

still those greenish brown eyes laughing a little
when i create some separation still
with what now seems indeed always was
a kind of winning grace in spades
i have always lacked which is why
i make promises i know i wont keep

inside this silly room in my head whose texture
is myriad mercifully brief cracks of light
in between bleeding visions of red blue
across a dingy black background

i hear that mans voice on the bloomfield bridge
black people need to wake up
we brothers & sisters need to get together

could be the insomnia saying
the black man is the original homo sapien my brother
see the black man invented the white man
its the truth young master
we dont know our history
if black people embraced our heritage

wed rule the world

*the world today is unnatural
it aint godly no no no it aint godly
look around*

*why you think the world so fucked up brother
cause it aint goldly no no no sir noooo
sir black people need to wake up
we brothers & sisters need to get together
we need to learn our history or else*

*the white man is gonna keep eating the cake
we making know what i mean
young master you a good brother
we need more brothers like you
my good brother you heard of allah the father
the holy & venerable father
 whats your name young master
what do they call you*

oh hes not so bad with his moony brown eyes
set deep in a face grim under moonlight
clearly ive tricked him he cant tell
im wasting this good golden bronze skin
ambivalent to the responsibility that comes with it
if only i could unzip & hand it over

so that a dutiful man who hears the call & responds
might wear it with dignity leaving me alone
in this silly dark room in my head
whose texture is myriad mercifully brief
cracks of light illuminating a roundtable
in the middle of a high school cafeteria

in between visions of red blue bleeding
across a dingy black background wherein

the joke is my bill cosby coogi sweater wearing
pudding pup loving receding hairline corny ass
say nigga like im a motherfuckin nursery school ass
white woman with a speech impediment
like stone sitting over there at the slow table
with his tongue tied ass

the joke is nigga give me that motherfuckin dorag
you dont even wear it right watch see
im white & i look blacker than you
with your even think about a tree & youll spark
a forest fire your ankles so ashy
you dont have no lotion ass
old ass looking nigga

the joke is i laugh along
when vino eats my lunch for me
laugh along as jeff kicks me until
i give him my ipod
laugh along when vino wont stop
pretending my skull is a catchers mitt
& his skittles are fast balls
laugh along when they call me oreo
laugh as long as the small cuts i make at night
with my mothers favorite steak knife

the joke is if when white people decide
to string up all the black boys one by one
& chuckle that we look like a patina
of mutant leaves on some dark october night
in omaha ne this white boyll get a noose

too i guess theres some comfort in knowing

on the other side of these myriad mercifully
brief cracks of light lies a chasm of deafening black
in which ones nerve endings soak in the warm
nothingness like in the first black chasm

red & blue bleeds through black
shadowy lips blow raspberries

thirty or so

when my bouquet of dew
freckled weeds were sunflowers
dazzling

& a breeze winked in passing
& her black iron door shut
its smoking lips &
the newly slick yellow
shimmered

bright green overgrowth
beneath pink cobble stones
lewd grasshoppers thunder

id go
nude to that green bed
riven by red spears

kiss the sun with
my golden bronze ass
one last flash of cheek
in evergreening maw
telling the moon
go for my throat

yes id go
back to be
another bright dead thing

**burned letter to birth mother: my private investigator
suggested i write down all the questions i want to ask you**

do you think of me
how often when why did you do you
experience regret or relief

how dare you how could you
would your kisses make me all better
do you did you why when how often

did you do you think if only i could go
back before everything changed
do their kisses make you all better

do my brother & sisters know
theyre the babies you chose
go back back back what would you

change that night that time that man
whats his name where can i find him
is he what was wrong with me

what was wrong with me
do you wonder
whats his name now
where can i find him
how do i go back

you dont

do you

*

my first boy
squirms & bites
he loves to leave me

i let him toddle
a few crab grass yards
pretend i dont see him
beneath a pile of orange
leaves finally lifting
his armpits with my talons

daddy fiddles his pipe
cheers his little man
under the porch
where a family of rats
bites back domestic felines
& coiled copperheads

mama strings a line of black overalls
shields her eyes from the sun
shining on her grandbaby boy
crawling with copperheads rats
& felines hiding seeking escape

not yet sweetheart not yet

twenty five

crows fat on the dead
& dying replace
fallen leaves

a murderous ensemble
the brisk black air rung
by their lovely crying

limbs of bur
swamp white oak
london plane mourning
in ebbing light

plumed heralds
squawking atop
a molting white oak
i climb &

nearly snatch one but
i slip & go to sleep on
a skirt of orange leaves

those red eyes
obliged to feast on what hides
in the company of leaves

fourteen

in middle school jamie jackson said
dillon thomas jones is a waste of black skin
i turned around like what the fuck you say

i said you a waste of black skin bitch
you talk white walk white everybody know
you white sooooo whats the problem look

believe me ive been hassling god for years like
sorry to bother you my man you made me black by mistake
hoping you get around to making a correction

i must not be worth his time which is to say
jamie i agree that i am failing to meet certain expectations
i suspect i will continue to fail

which will prove bothersome
for both black folk & myself
for yall my presence suggests
a certain material indeterminacy
of blackness whose assumed stability
is the foundation of black identity
leaving me agonizingly adrift
in said material indeterminacy

ive found relief at the bottom of the nearest

bottle of rum which tastes better than
cutting my inner thighs open although

both defang my paralyzing
existential ambivalence
which is to say

jamie i dont feel in control of who i am

i suspect ill always feel at the mercy of
judicious people like yourself

know no matter what happens
ill always remember you said

to mariah johnston loud enough so i heard
who & what i was slash am as you saw me
in relation to you then & henceforward

dillon thomas jones
a waste of black skin

twentysix

nobuyukis lacquer sculpture womb
two black two red & three more black
layers of lampblack & cinnabar
dyed lacquer skin six foot ten

garish brow lit by blinkered
white fluorescent lights
luscious black black red red
black black black five foot
three wide red ring says
keep your distance

i circle this opened
black blade of water falling
in blinkered light

penetrable as the belly of the cave
in my dreams the womb i once
knew harvested polished
preserved for posterity

for this moment of longing desire
to enter delicious black surface
lose give up off myself imagine
recomposed as this outer side
skin impenetrable impossibly
black nothing beyond

inner side temperature controlled
reddish flesh my long fingers
break a boundary

reach back towards
a room of shadows
breaking the bluest
eyes white knuckle
grip round my gasping
throat

i slough two black two red
& three more black layers
of lampblack & cinnabar
dyed lacquer skin beneath
white fluorescent glowering
ebony agate sent aground

whats left is thick vermillion streaks
layered drips of sunset set against
god awful white light beating back

black black black

sixteen or so

tilt your head
trip orange lamp
light into brown
black holes

what might
happen next
might not

pin each lip corner
to an earlobe
hold til dry
pink lips tear

chuckle
a flicked knife

what shell do next
she might not

look over your shoulder
til you hear a pop
keep turning

what will be
will be what
you decide

rest your chin
on your black fist

burned letter to birth mother: tell my father if you see him

coach parks says
when white people round up
all the black men in america
theyll loop a knot for me too

coach parks says
a man needs sex like oxygen
my dick better meet expectations

coach parks says
i am the talented tenth
i must lift up the black race
if i marry a white woman
im a race traitor

coach parks never does teach me
to box he does not always pick up
or call back when i leave a message
anoints himself my black male role model

the father he says
every young black boy needs
if you see him tell my father
when coach parks says *son*
his mouth smells like a light rain
soaked tomato garden

tell my father
i call coach parks *dad*
when he one arm hugs me
behind his back
i cross my fingers

*

your daddy is a single twenty year old
black man who did what he wanted
my freshman year

he & cherise were going together
she saw how he stretched my quads
broke my ankle with a hurtle

hes doing his thing in college
franklin or dominican
dont know what he studies
dont know about his dreams

know i wasnt the last girl
cherise fought for him
know he about five nine
weighs less than my daddy

dont know anything about his people
figure they just regular black folk
with their own blues

im sure he fears god &
takes what he wants
like my daddy your daddy
pulled me down after prom

spring freshman year
cherise saw my ankles behind my ears
your daddys hard sloping back

thirty two

amble down pink
cobblestone toward
the latched wooden gate
footsteps
a stranger follows

out of the place i left
into a field of sundrunk
dandelions chanting *run*
run   run

a skip here a hop
there is all i can manage
five years old skipping
while my skin cooks

twenty years gone
still three away
her hand molesting
my shadow dogged breath
my dripping nape

run   run   run
beyond the reach of
white strangulations
strain three two
one click

my mother made breakfast
eggs on the patio
pink cobblestones go
beyond unlatched gates
where children gallop

*

i won the ohio state high school
one hundred meter dash
eight months pregnant

coach mac said
i had god given talent
flawless technique
called me flojo

lines of sad little girls sucking air
jaws slack knees shaking
in the dust i whipped up
day in day out
checking my shining teeth
in red nails six inches long

sad little girls
bent over starting blocks
dripping dreading
the big bang

coach mac said
i dont care i dont care
god made you
flawless

devour these sad little girls

six

a dying star trapped
in a popcorn ceiling
crooked wind blown
through swiss mesh white
moonlit waves black
against the closets teeth

a coterie of beanie babies
chokes on dust in the corner
the floor is a tarpit specially
made to split & spit
sunflower seeds

marlboro white tentacles
from the doorways elbow
campbell v8 splash
dollar store vodka
her red spit up
on my blueberry bedframe

the white walls keep quiet
new coats each year
for good behavior
bleary eyes witness
v8 vodka spatter

what flutters fleetingly
through the unhurried mind of
this dutiful mattress

during my nightly humiliation
beneath these red rocketships
on white cotton sheets

who knows where &
how long the hard line is
the night flashes
its tattered green slip
haggard springs pump
with their eyes closed
urine is sticky
tape between my toes
it hurts

less than zero to five

one evening during dinner
my chest splits open
revealing a tract of
grey smoke white noise

an essence of a person exists
mine is one hand reaching for
the black bottom of blue water
forever never quite touching
while the other hand asks santa
for a black hole to spit me out
in the universe where
my birth mother kept me

id cut the throat of another five year old self
haul him to another mothers dinner table
kiss him on the forehead
wish him much luck

hell scream scream
& scream until no one notices
hes dead at dinner

i scour the smoke
there is no origin no end

burned letter to birth mother: when i was five my mother told me all about you

another woman spit you out
i wanted you
she didnt want you
understand

i didnt carry you in my belly but
im your mother
i wanted you

shes black
youre black
im white

i love you
she didnt love you
you still love me dont you

nobody wanted you
i wanted you
she didnt love you

understand
another woman spit you out
i wanted you
she didnt want you

*

couldnt stop making you making you making you

on bed rest in november belting
he fills me up he gives me love
more love than ive ever seen

went parttime at lazams until
i couldnt stand long or needed help
pulling my blue electric leggings up
over my bee stung swollen feet

in bed eyes closing every few thomas & beluah
poems tried a shift to the color purple
couldnt read sethes letters without
needing to release my bladder meaning
i might have to pass daddy in the hallway so

i switched to beloved dreamt of you writing
letters lost in an underwater underworld dreamt
you waiting to hear from me until fed up
you lay down on the front porch daddy finds you

makes me spell goodbye across your slick throat
with his woodcarving knife as if i dont know
the way to stop making you requires metal
sharp & silver

i dreamt of unmaking you all night long
mariah belting *he fills me up he gives me love*

*

how momma didnt sense
daddys weight leave her

when she knew without seeing
who slammed the front door
what mood they carried
why not the thunderstorm
daddy roused rumbling
night stand to night stand

night after
night after
night after

fried eggs yolk running
nails tickling the nape of his neck
every morning after
he pinned my ankles
behind my ears
struck my cheeks with
his big man sweat

night after night
after night
after night

four years
every night she kissed both my cheeks

how
i never ask her

*

i got hot at the sound of your first wail
a soup of rage bubbled in my belly
i was too hot to touch you

couldnt give your baby heart heat stroke
saw your new fingers new toes go limp
what a waste to die so soon
seeing as you took all that time to cook

so what if momma begged pleaded
hollered about me & my selfish ways
couldnt understand why i wouldnt
torch a brand new life i made

tamarra understood kept her back turned
while she rocked you so i couldnt
get used to the curve of your smile
couldnt register you squinted
the way i squint when at a crossroads

i saw you swaddled in daddys big arms
& blink blinked to confirm
you & him shared a nose threw the bible
threw the bedside table at him
you touch me again
your bonesll catch flame

burned letter to birth mother: bedtime storytime two

i see white yellow teeth bared
red rimmed eyes a red tongue lolling

theres a monster at the end of this poem

when her head droops i steal a sip
turn my eye red my eye red my tongue red

in a mirror i see red marks on my white teeth

she slurs i fetch another boxed wine from her closet
blood flushes my cheeks numb to pinches

theres a monster at the end of this poem

she demands i correct my childish behavior
in the near future resolves not to raise a devil

i peer through the tears trapped in my eye & notice

her body folds over itself from her mouth
a light red puddle of spittle wets the pages of

another monster at the end of this book

on nights she prowls the living room i sentry
in her shadow bright eyes gleaming teeth
reddened my mother whimpers wildly

i feast on my own heart

burned letter to birth mother: blink

blink & youll miss the boy
behind my eyes pushing
red about white linoleum

between gulps of *franzia merlot*
his mother insists *something went wrong
inside her womb* cup after cup

into the crestfallen evening
the boy learns his essence is
she did not want you
something went wrong
in the womb what why how

questions unanswered consume
the light in his eyes what is intrinsic
rendered inaccessible unless one

braves the maze of moats & fire traps
beneath the transylvanian fortress
constructed around him care taken

to misdirect from the truth behind
my spike studded brown eyes

youll find a boy sweeping *franzia
merlot* about white linoleum

thirteen

snow cheeks splotched
red cleaver wet
mint blade a glint
the butcher liberates
a soul

blood flecks dry on lips
red velvet pool paints toes
glistening wrists teach

slaughter as reduction
out with bone skin fat
blood drains

cleave open deadened life
bag & tie what sells
out with the rest

despite exquisite instruction
my knife yet lacks
a clean edge

i slice skin
puncture vein
break bone
harvest heart
black cheeks
flush bloodred

red splatter *drip*
*drip plop*s red

red red

twenty nine

seems a good night to leave
this sodden black body behind
fling my name into the light

tingling fingers cocksure
coursing with bitter rage
fumble with a bighearted blade

survived the pills the booze
still daily i dream of reprieve
a black convulsion
at the close of day

of white wisps
my extinguished flame
of a good night like this
my gentle right hand
spills my life
into a dream

dear you fools who loved me
know i went gently into a black sky
brimming with dying light

my raging particles of dust
went gently yes gently
finally free from given names
it was a goodgood night

twenty eight

a goodyear tire
its thick black neck
hanged by white rope

my boyhood swing
evergreen leaves keeping sunlight
inside its black belly

tied to the oak in the front yard
swinging this way &that
shrouded in vanishing sunlight

we moved one day i came back
wizened but upright
swaying this way &that

oak & rope remain
god willing
their blinds are drawn

so why not me instead of
this goodyear tire
god willing
the rope will hold

burned letter to birth mother: if youre reading this its too late

every day i wait
you never come
were never coming
every day i need you
youre not here

every night my mother sees
red blue eyed black holes
swallow light swallow me
every day whats left is

bone skin sputtering
blood below moonlight
its too late

i forgive you
just kidding
too late

dont care what
dont care why
too late

too late ill die
unforgiving
when i needed you
you werent there

*

ill be in the belly of some great house
dusting gold frames of my sons
smiling face on the mantle
telling myself to toss
an old name in the fire

next to daddys granddaddys piano
with the carved faces of slaves for legs
because our past is with us
framed in light flashes stomach knots
& wisps of vibrating syllables
catching me by surprise

sitting in the parlor
watching dust dancing in sunlight
blown through french doors
my son kicked open the last night
he left hasnt been back since

ill wait for a man to rise
out of the ohio river &
lay on my porch drying
in sunlight

ill place his cheek on my breast
answer his questions satisfy
the anger he gives me
he grows strong i fall weak

needing the child i named
& sent into the sky to let me
toss his name into the fire

leave me to suffer the anger of
the only son i have left
in this great empty nest
light bleached rooms choking
on dust beneath which
golden smiles wait to bloom

elegy

boy little oh five one six one nine
mayme park twenty seventh year
a thursday twenty first century
the pittsburgh epoch
a spring like summer

aka jones t   dillon
seasoned grifter of
boorish half truths &
sentimental claptrap
what it is it is now

scatter sunflower petals about
the trunk of this oak tree or
schenley parks stone covered belly
where he washed his bones
in the shadow of a bluish mound
knee bent to ground
this blue bit of water
this domesticated groove of
cut granite white runoff
desiccated sunlight lances

drive to south eighty eighth street
where it all happened where
the scars grew thick with blood
strips of a baby blue baby blanket
lindas wet face red & red
& wet as *franzia sunset blush*
a green lawn nails filed polished
for what was it   twenty dollars
an oak tree tied to a firestone tire swing

mommy please come save me
she cannot hear you
frasier mash walker texas ranger
will & grace friends
endless assault of blinkered lights
cold rough hands in a warm bed
a bag of dandelion heads
a harried baby blue baby blanket
bequeathed to whoever wants it
its seen some things let me tell you

haymarket pedestrian bridge
a once upon a time final resting place
marcos nosy mouth invasive breath
a crying nose   it was a cold night
wearing a birthday suit
loosened necktie receding hairline
twentyish year leftfoot brown sperry topsider
right foot brown alden driving loafer
black belt with white varicose veins

pawn shop wedding ring for your magda
garbage can carnation matching black wayfarers
leticias yellow lace handkerchief
life measured with a stiff upper lip
& flasks of kentucky bourbon

one page memorial program
church fan set upon by moths
hearse with a shotgun engine
white clouds overhead cover
the heart with black falling leaves
dont they

sudden blue jay song
they used to come around & sing
purple sunset humping
bare brown branches
citadel of fireflies
dead on the windowsill

sinuous sprinkler bending its spray in the front yard
red lawn mower copper teeth aching for an arm
leg foot   white stars red stripes
death flagging in the cool breeze
a bloody bicyclist limped away
i swore id never tell

through her heavy black door
my stilted black gait

summer of everclear & one fifty one rum
kool & the gangs emergency on repeat
all i can produce is the taste of dust on that windowsill
collected during years of yearning
against glass   pliant mesh
a plastic bag articulates
a change in the direction

called her by her sisters name
how easy fingers slop a long
carefully cut sex line
strongly recommend crabcakes for
pleasurable edification   dreaming

a field of reeds are gnashing anacondas
nothing compares to the ecstasy of

sunlight poring over my naked body
grassy knoll beneath some elm by love library

the black silk shawl lapel of that dinner jacket
black comb teeth slick with american crew pomade
never did learn the art of breathing properly
luckily i keep a spare dillon thomas jones in the boot

funny thing about her eyes
they never sparkle
folds of flesh swallow
taupe spandex

circling gnats a kind of crown
put away the castanets
christsake

this is a eulogy
i declare myself
winner of all unsettled feuds
may my foes struggle to survive
the coming floods

i bought you a stamp in lisbon
even after you said no
thank you for the thought
& the gesture

goodbye bologna & swiss sandwiches cut in triangles
without crust
goodbye milky way caramels
goodbye salted peanuts in rosenblatts blue metal chairs
goodbye aunt loris corn casserole clogging my veins
deliciously

goodbye gus the spider plant the only thing alive in
this room

the moss creeping the linoleum
a shadow or mold i think
whatever the hungry caterpillar ate

if death were a kind of cocoon then
a loose thread looped tight round a finger
blood desperately seeking oxygen
red fingers in sweaty armpits
one last sweet smoldering cigarette stub

a cornhusker quarter
heads or tails
twenty vicodin or
twenty xanax

shouldve got magda a veil
even if for a laugh shouldve respected
the moment before tragedy

always been a one size fits all kind of guy
the pattern is im the one who doesnt fit
sign here agree to go quietly in dark
one knowing shoulder squeeze suffices

to faiz i bequeath my first place trophies
who will i widow
who will count themselves my survivors
in whose hand the handle of a golden shovel
& what of the pulley
only black gloves please
next to charlies bones if you could

this may require arbitration

im the scarab clutching your right earlobe
dillon thomas jones poet or whatever
currently seeking employment
in another version of life

the brief crack of light on the tail side of a rusted nickel
where folk sneeze with their eyes wide open
try it

a cough is a gauche confession of
ones inability to suppress the bodies
grotesque animality

this is a pathetic attempt to violate
lindas lien upon my soul
tonyas cocoa butter hand in mayme park
half shade lighter than mine
half shade lighter than my uncle
my grandfather

she said i had no right to walk the brick pathway
shouldve turned back at the curb
shouldve walked to the two story ranch
on eighty eighth street

wide peeling feet
spine a compressed column of
red dust

chest
a brief crack of light

notes acknowledgements

all the poems are written in what im calling loose terzanelle a variation on the villanelle

originally the poems were traditional terzanelle in prose blocks

this made them appear to be prose poems with the internal structure hidden

it was cute & when it worked well it worked well but when it didnt the poems were too weak

in their loosened form the structure is still there but im no longer hiding behind it

the age poems are riffs on a poem called five written by a poet whose name i thought id always remember turns out i forgot

in the poem the poet addresses her five year old self

she lets her child self know they make it to twenty five

i think

i cant find the poem and i cant remember the poet

at one time i had the collection of poems this poem is in but i let a friend borrow it &
they never gave it back

plus im not friends with that person anymore so

this person im no longer friends with i remember we spoke a lot about this project during
its second phase during which time i wasnt pushing myself far enough we both knew
that but they thought i should go one direction & i thought i should go another way

i went my own way which was the correct decision

my decision to go my own way with this project during what i call its second phase is not all that related to the dissolution of said friendship

but i would say they helped me understand that we generally saw things differently
initially stimulating then boring because they were often incorrect

especially about my book but they were influential so herein i acknowledge them

dr marianne kunkel showed us the poem five by the poet i cant remember whose book i gave to a one time friend etc
dr kunkel was the first person to encourage me to write poetry

she was one of the first people i talked to about searching for my birth mother when i started searching eight years ago

i wrote six & nine in her class eight years ago

ive been revising them for eight years

i started writing this book eight years ago

in some ways ive spent my life thus far writing this book

finishing was the one thing i felt i must do i must finish this no matter what

i always felt the point of my life the point at the end of the arch of my life was this book & then my life would end

kind of like theres a monster at the end of this book which is referenced in bedtime storytime one & two in a way that makes sense to me in terms of feeling

the tonya poems are persona poems in which i imagine my birth mother

her voice is one part sethe from the color purple one part thomas & beulah one part beloved one part other stuff

in a poetry seminar willie kinard three suggested i call one of my poems burned letter to birth mother

thanks to willie for real that was genius

thanks to kate peter faiz olivia missy sam josh tom

thanks to marianne & kwame

thanks to tyler bill & yona

thanks to paul

thanks to jenny

thanks to tj & pauline

also elegy is a poem built around on top of a structure provided by tjs poem how to be remembered

cute right

thanks to the indianapolis review   coal hill review   yemassee   the iowa review online
the shore   & the florida review

thanks to josh for asking me about my book and sending it to david

thanks to david for fucking with my vision

thanks to julia for designing the perfect cover & on the first try no less

mega thanks to abigail for being the perfect person to edit this book

& the most thanks in the world to yasmine
this book doesnt exist with out you

now im fine if the plane crashes

ill smile

up in flames

lauren k alleyne

Dillon Thomas Jones is a writer living in Pittsburgh, PA. He holds a BA in English (Creative Writing) from the University of Nebraska-Lincoln and an MFA in Creative Writing from the University of Pittsburgh. He writes poetry, fiction and cultural criticism about television, film and books. His work has appeared in *Yemessee*, The *Indianapolis Review*, *Coal Hill Review*, *The Iowa Review*, and *The Shore*.

www.ingramcontent.com/pod-product-compliance
Lightning Source LLC
Chambersburg PA
CBHW020913080526
44589CB00011B/574